ASSEMBLY OF GOD
SUNDAY SCHOOL
CAIRNBULG

Presented to

HEATHER CASSIE

30/3/86

CONQUEROR OF DARKNESS

CONQUEROR OF DARKNESS

The Story of Helen Keller

by
PHYLLIS GARLICK

LUTTERWORTH PRESS
GUILDFORD AND LONDON

First published 1958
Second impression 1960
Third impression 1962
Fourth impression 1963
Fifth impression 1966
Sixth impression 1969
Seventh impression 1972
Eighth impression 1977
Ninth impression 1981

ISBN 0 7188 0865 7

PRINTED IN GREAT BRITAIN
BY MACKAYS OF CHATHAM LTD

CONTENTS

1

"LET ME OUT!"

ON a farm in Alabama, in the southern States of America, Helen Keller was growing up in a strange world of her own. It was this strangeness, this being different from everybody else, that infuriated her. On this lovely morning in the early summer of 1886 she might have been having the greatest fun playing with Belle, her big setter, and the other animals on the farm, or hunting for guinea fowl eggs with Martha Washington, the cook's little girl. Instead she was in one of her blackest, most difficult moods. She had raged and kicked out at Martha until the poor child took to her heels and rushed into the kitchen for safety, knowing from bitter experience who would have the best of a hand to hand encounter.

And now Helen was fighting it out by herself—the frustrated, wretched feeling of wanting to do things just like other people and not being able to do them. At last, her rage worked off in kicks and sobs and pounding the grass with her clenched fist, she rolled over on her back and turned her face to the sky. She felt the warm breeze run over

7

her bare arms and legs, and she caught the scent of jasmine and the roses clustered over the porch of the house. But she could see nothing, she could hear nothing.

Helen Keller was blind.

She was stone deaf.

And because she was stone deaf she was unable to speak.

Yet she was bursting with life and energy. But because she could neither see nor hear nor speak, it was all bottled up inside her instead of finding an outlet in the thousand and one exciting ways that ordinary people know. Her black moods, her stormy outbursts of temper were the result; as though all the life and energy in her were hammering on a closed door and shouting: "Let me out! Let me out!"

*   *   *

Helen Keller had not started life by being different from anyone else. She was born in the June of 1880, a healthy, normal baby, the first of the family. At eighteen months she was very advanced for her age, quick and intelligent, imitating all that she saw other people do. She was ahead of most children in learning to talk a little. One of the first words she tried to say in her own way was "water". She loved the garden with its masses of roses and honeysuckle and the Southern smilax, the haunt of bees and humming-birds. Her favourite spot was the summer house at the far end; it was covered by a beautiful vine and with trailing clematis, a special place to play.

Suddenly those happy days came to an end. When she was barely two Helen was taken ill, so ill that the doctor thought she could not live. Her parents were terribly upset. How quiet the house and garden seemed without the sound of running feet and Helen's prattling tongue!

But one morning the fever left her as suddenly as it had come. After all it seemed that she might soon be up and running about again. Then the sad truth began to dawn on the doctor and on Captain and Mrs. Keller. As a result of the illness, Helen had lost the power both to see and to hear. She heard nothing when they spoke to her; she moved her lips but no sound came. Though her eyes were open she could see nothing when they held up her toys or when the dog sat down beside her. She could only feel things with her hands.

From that time Helen had to live shut up inside herself, in a silent, lonely world of her own. At first she clung helplessly to her mother, holding on to her dress while she went about her work. But gradually she began to find her own way about and to discover means of making herself half understood. A shake of her head meant "No", a nod "Yes", a pull meant "Come", and a push

"Go". When she wanted bread she imitated the act of cutting a loaf and buttering the slices. She loved ice cream and when she wanted her mother to make some for dinner she made the sign for working the freezer and shivered as though with the cold.

Her mother and Martha Washington, the little coloured girl, quickly understood her miming. And Helen herself grew to understand a good deal of what was going on around her. She felt every object with her hands and learned what things were by the feel of them. At five she could fold and put away her own clothes when they came back from the laundry, able to distinguish her own from the rest. She always knew when her mother was going out by the feel of her clothes and made it clear that she wanted to be taken too.

Her fingers were her eyes, in the house and out of doors. She knew all the animals and livestock on their large farm. She liked to feel the hens and turkeys taking food from her hand; to stroke the smooth coats and arching necks of the horses in the stables; to be with the cows at milking time, to smell their warm breath and to feel along their velvety flanks.

Besides her sensitive touch Helen's keen sense of smell helped to guide her too. The warm, appetizing smell of baking would draw her to the kitchen just at the right time when Martha's mother was taking a tasty batch of cookies out of the oven. Though she was often very much in the way, Cook was kind and humoured her and let her help by kneading the dough, grinding the spices and picking over the raisins, ending up with a sly licking of the stirring spoons!

But it was out in the garden that Helen's sense of smell helped her specially to find her way about. She would feel along the square stiff box-wood hedges, following the scent of the flowers to find the first violets and lilies. She found her own way too to the summer house by the scent of its particular flowers as well as by the feel of leaves and blossom.

When visitors came to "Ivy Green", Helen was always sent for to meet them. She was not at all shy; in fact she rather enjoyed being in the limelight. On one occasion she surpassed herself by putting on what she considered "company" dress for a special visitor who had called. She rushed upstairs, smothered her face with powder, draped a veil over her head and tied a huge bustle round her waist, then descended to help entertain the somewhat astonished male visitor.

The Kellers kept open house for all their friends. Captain Keller, who had served in the Confederate Army during the Civil War, hardly ever came home without bringing a guest. He was a keen sportsman and was renowned in the neighbourhood as a fine shot and as the owner of a great many dogs.

Helen was made much of by the guests as well as by her parents. With her strong personality she practically ruled the household until the coming of a younger sister, Mildred. At first she resented the demands Mildred made on her mother's attention, but she became very fond of her as she grew up.

Though it was not surprising that Helen was spoilt, it made her extremely difficult. She fought like a tiger to get what she wanted, and lorded it over the more biddable Martha Washington. When they went egg hunting together and were lucky enough to find a guinea fowl's nest in the long grass, Helen always insisted on carrying the eggs home herself, making it clear to Martha by very emphatic signs that *she* would be sure to fall and break them. Anyone less good tempered than Martha would have found Helen a trying companion. But it was difficult for people not to spoil her since she was cut off from so much ordinary fun and enjoyment.

As it was, she and Martha shared a great propensity for getting into scrapes together. One hot summer afternoon they were sitting on the veranda steps cutting out paper dolls. They soon grew tired of this and after cutting up their shoestrings Helen turned the scissors on Martha's fuzzy little black corkscrew curls. Martha then seized the scissors and had just cut off the first of Helen's long, fair curls when fortunately Mrs. Keller appeared and put a stop to the game!

★ ★ ★

In spite of occasional fun and mischief, Helen was becoming increasingly lonely and unhappy. It was dawning on her how different she was from other people.

She knew that her mother and her friends never used the kind of signs she had to make when she wanted anything done. They talked with their lips. Yet when she stood between two people who were talking and touched their lips she could not understand at all what they were saying, and this made her very angry. She tried moving her own lips and frantically making signs, but it was no use. She could not understand them. They could not understand her. In her rage against her helplessness she kicked and screamed till she was tired out and utterly miserable.

Their friends and neighbours were full of sympathy for Helen and her parents.

"Poor Helen Keller," the grown-ups said among themselves. "And to think that nothing can be done for her! How can she ever make anything of life? What *will* it be like for her when she grows up! If she can neither talk to people nor read books, how can her mind develop, and how can she possibly find anything useful to do?"

Though the children who played with Helen accepted her quite naturally and did their best to understand the signs she made, as soon as she started one of her tantrums they went off and left her to herself. But sometimes a friend with more imagination than the rest tried hard to picture what it must feel like to be blind and deaf like Helen. She would say to herself, "I'm shutting my eyes tight and sticking my fingers in my ears, and I'll pretend I can't talk—oh dear, I can't keep it up for long, though."

She knew that for her it was just a game. She had only to open her eyes, unstop her ears, and all the friendly, homely sights of green fields and garden, the roof tops of the little country town of Tuscumbia, and the over-arching blue sky, the song of the birds and the shouts of other children at play would come rushing in again.

But it could never be like that for Helen Keller.

As her violent outbursts steadily increased, Captain and Mrs. Keller were at a loss to know what to do.

"If Helen goes on like this," said her father sadly, "she will become more and more unhappy, a trial to herself and to everyone else. But how can we find a way of helping her? Everyone takes it for granted that it's impossible for her to be taught.

And even if we could hear of a teacher, who would want to come to an out of the way little country town like this?"

Mrs. Keller carefully folded the pair of Helen's socks she had been mending, and said thoughtfully: "You know, I keep thinking of that girl, Laura Bridgman, whom Charles Dickens wrote about. She was the first deaf and blind person in the world ever to be taught. Do you remember it was a Dr. Samuel Howe who found a way of teaching her?"

"Yes," said her husband, "but didn't he die some years ago? How do we know that anyone else is able to carry on his methods now? We are so off the map anyway, nowhere near any school for the blind or the deaf."

All the same, Captain Keller made up his mind that if they heard of anyone who could really advise them what to do, he would spare neither time nor money in getting the best possible help for Helen. So when news reached them soon after this of a famous eye specialist in Baltimore who had dealt successfully with many seemingly hopeless cases, they decided at once to take Helen to see him.

She was thrilled with the long journey and made friends with several people on the train. Her aunt made her a big shapeless and featureless doll out of towels tied together. Helen at once pointed to where the eyes should be and made signs to have some put in. No one seemed equal to the task, till Helen herself had a bright idea. She searched under the seat and found her aunt's cape which was trimmed with large beads. She pulled off two and made signs that she wanted to have them sewn on to her doll. When this was done she was happy. Throughout the long journey she showed no sign of temper. Now that her mind and fingers were occupied, she had no need to let off steam in outbursts of rage and rebellion.

When they saw the doctor in Baltimore he examined Helen's eyes very carefully. Then he shook his head sadly. "No, I am afraid nothing can be done about her blindness," he said to her parents. "But," he added, "she can be taught. I advise you to consult Dr. Alexander Graham Bell of Washington. He can tell you all about schools and teachers of deaf or blind children."

They went on at once to Washington, Helen full of excitement at travelling from place to place; Captain and Mrs. Keller desperately hoping that some good might come of the visit.

Dr. Bell was a great man, famous as the inventor of the telephone. He was also a noted specialist for the deaf and dumb. As he held out his watch for Helen to feel, and took her on his knee, she knew at once that he was a friend. He understood the signs she made and that gave her confidence.

He turned to her father. "She *can* be taught,"

he said. "I advise you to write to the Perkins Institute in Boston—where Dr. Howe carried on his great work for the blind. I know you've read of Laura Bridgman and the way he was able to teach her? Well, ask the present head of the Institute if he has a teacher he can recommend to begin Helen's education."

Captain Keller lost no time in writing to ask. A few weeks later he received a letter with the great news that someone with an outstanding gift for teaching the blind was ready to come to them. Her name was Anne Sullivan. She herself had been almost totally blind for a time. She had been educated at the Perkins Institute where she came to know Laura Bridgman. Now that she had partially recovered her sight, and had graduated with distinction at the age of twenty-one, she meant to devote her life to teaching blind children.

The news of her coming to Ivy Green was the first hint of light about to break in on Helen's darkness.

2

THE DOOR OPENS

ON the spring day in 1887 when Anne Sullivan was due to arrive to begin Helen's education, there was an air of suppressed excitement about the entire household. So much was going to depend on her. Could she possibly succeed in teaching this wild little creature who was getting beyond anyone's power to control?

Helen had guessed from her mother's signs and from the general hurrying to and fro that something unusual was afoot. Someone important must be coming. She ran out to the porch and stood on the steps waiting impatiently for her mother to come back from the station with the visitor.

Suddenly she felt approaching footsteps. She rushed towards Anne Sullivan, felt her face and dress, snatched her bag and tried to open it. If she could have read Anne Sullivan's thoughts at that moment she would have known what a surprise it was to her new teacher to find instead of the pale, delicate child she had imagined, a healthy, boisterous six-year-old, wild and restive as a forest pony.

Helen's tireless activity was almost the first thing that struck Anne Sullivan. She was never still for a moment and her hands were in everything. That first evening Helen insisted on helping Anne unpack and put away her things. She tried on Anne's bonnet and cocked her head in front of the glass just as though she could see.

Anne watched her with sympathy as well as amusement. She could see that Helen's quick, restless movements were not those of a happy, contented child.

"She has untaught, unsatisfied hands," she thought to herself. And she longed to get started on teaching her by the hand alphabet method she had learned at the Institute—those simple movements of fingers and hand by which deaf people can spell words into each other's hands, at great speed. If blind and deaf Laura Bridgman could learn to talk with her fingers, and to read and write, why should not Helen do the same?

Anne had brought with her in her trunk a doll which the blind children at the Institute had sent as a present for Helen. (It had been specially dressed for her by Laura Bridgman, though Helen did not understand this at the time.) After she had played with it, Anne spelt into Helen's hand the word "d-o-l-l".

Helen was at once interested in this finger play and tried to imitate it. Without in the least understanding that she was spelling a word—or even that there were such things—she went on imitating her teacher. The next word was "cake". Anne held out the cake to Helen while she wrote "cake" into her free hand.

Helen had had her first lesson, spelt out her first two words.

★   ★   ★

But there were difficulties innumerable and many stormy scenes as the lessons went on. At one moment Helen would seem interested, the next she would grow impatient and fly into a rage, and become completely unteachable. Her table manners were appalling. She grabbed food from other people's plates and when Anne refused to let her take food from her plate she flung herself on the floor, kicking and screaming and trying to pull Anne's chair from under her.

That "scene", which was one of many, decided Anne Sullivan. She could see that Helen was utterly spoilt. For the sake of peace the family had let her do exactly as she pleased. The only hope now of controlling and teaching her without breaking her spirit was to have Helen on her own for a little while, away from her home and over-indulgent family.

Fortunately Captain and Mrs. Keller agreed to the experiment Anne suggested. She and Helen went to live all by themselves in an attractive little garden-house a quarter of a mile away. Their meals were sent to them from the big house and every day Captain and Mrs. Keller looked in at the window to see how they were getting on.

At first the terrific tussles continued, but gradually the new plan began to work. Helen quietened down. She learned to use her hands, to string beads, to knit and to crochet a little, to make an apron for her doll, as well as to learn new words which Anne spelt into her hand. When one morning her dog Belle came to see them, Helen sat down by her and began to work the dog's claws. Having first spelt the word "doll" on her own fingers she was trying to teach Belle to spell it too.

When they went back to Ivy Green, everyone was struck with the difference in Helen. She was beginning to be much less difficult to manage because she was happier and had some new interests.

Day after day Anne Sullivan taught her new words with much patience and ingenuity. She would first give her the object to feel, then spell the name for it into her hand. (For each letter there was a special position for the fingers and the hand.) At the end of a month Helen had learned eighteen nouns and three verbs and was eager for more. But she still did not understand what she was doing. She was only learning to imitate mechanically Anne's finger play for each new word.

Then suddenly light dawned.

One morning she was very impatient over two new words which she muddled up—mug and water. To avoid a further scene indoors, Anne took her down the garden to continue the lesson out in the sunshine. When they came to the pump-house Anne made Helen hold her mug under the spout while she pumped. Then as the cool stream gushed out, filling the mug and running over Helen's arm, her teacher spelt "water" several times into her free hand.

Helen dropped the mug and stood there in sudden astonishment. A new light of understanding came into her face. This cool stream had a name; it was water. For her it was a special word, one that she had tried to say long ago before her illness.

All the way back to the house she was hopping and dancing with excitement. Everything had a name. Now she wanted to know the name of every object she touched—beginning with Anne herself who spelled into her hand "Teacher". In a few hours Helen had learned thirty new words.

It was a great day both for her and her teacher. Helen went to bed so thrilled with this new experience that for the first time she showed some real affection for Anne and kissed her good night for gladness.

*　　*　　*

The most wonderful thing in the world had happened to Helen Keller. From that moment in the well-house when she suddenly understood the meaning of the word "water" her mind had come awake for the first time. It was as though a closed door had been magically opened. Now she was taking her first running steps through it into an exciting new world. To know that everything she touched had a name made her tingle with excitement to find out more and more by exploring with her fingers and then getting Anne to tell her the name of the object. What a thrill it was to learn the names of those closest to her, mother, father, baby Mildred, Cousin Leila and her little girls, Martha Washington and the rest. Those first words and names she learned, knowing what they meant, were like beams of light in the darkness of not knowing or understanding the real world about her.

The light spread the more she learned, and she learned very quickly. Anne was very clever at playing the game of "touch and tell" by which Helen came to know the names of things and their uses. In making a game of it she was teaching Helen for the first time how to play—and how to laugh. One morning Anne and Mrs. Keller came into the room much amused at something that had happened. Anne was laughing gaily and in her longing for Helen to be able to join in too she put the child's hand on her own puckered up face while she spelt "laugh", then tickled her so that instinctively Helen laughed too. It was the first time she had ever laughed since she became blind and deaf as a baby. No wonder the family was thrilled.

The exploring went on, all day every day, touching, handling everything that came her way. The more her knowledge of things grew, the more delight Helen took in the world about her. The feel of a blade of grass, of the smooth or knotted trunk of a tree in the woods, the soft curve of her baby sister's cheek—she had a name for them all now, and was beginning to build up a picture of things in her own mind.

One morning when she was playing in the garden she wandered into the pump-house. She felt a cold nose snuffling against her hand and bent down to pat the setter lying in the corner. Much to her surprise she felt several warm bodies pushing against her hand. Then she felt them snuggle against their mother to be fed. In great excitement she rushed indoors to tell Anne. She kept spelling "dog-baby" and pointing to her five fingers, sucking each one in turn.

Anne's first thought was that one of the dogs had hurt Mildred, the baby. But when Helen led her out to the pump-house, she saw lying there in the corner the new family of five puppies which had caused such excitement. For the first time Helen had been able to convey in a word or two news of a great event.

She was a different person now that her mind was beginning to grow. Every day her face grew more expressive, happy and contented. Anne Sullivan was a wonderful teacher and gave a great deal of thought to the best way of helping Helen to learn. She began now to talk into her hand in complete sentences instead of single words, just as she would to any child who could hear.

They went for long rambles together, through the fields and woods, and all the time Helen asked endless questions about the world she could not see but about which she was now beginning to know a little. These lessons out of doors satisfied her longing for action as well as her thirst for knowledge.

Playing on the banks of the Tennessee River she learned of the way things grow out of the ground, how the birds live and build their nests, how the squirrels and the deer and other living creatures find food and shelter. Her favourite walk with Anne was to Keller's Landing—the old lumber wharf on the river, used as a landing-place for soldiers during the Civil War. Here she learned to build dams of pebbles, made islands and lakes and dug river-beds without in the least realizing that this was in fact a geography lesson!

One warm spring morning they were returning from a long ramble feeling rather hot and tired for the weather had turned close and sultry. They stopped for a rest in the shade of a wild cherry tree not far from home. Anne helped Helen to climb up to a cool perch among the branches. Then she had an idea. Why not have a picnic lunch here instead of going indoors? She would go back to the house for some food if Helen promised to stay where she was and not move from her seat in the branches.

Helen promised and settled down to wait. After a bit she felt a sudden chill in the air and she knew that the sun had gone in. Then her quick sense of smell told her that the particular scent rising from the earth meant that a thunder-storm was near. She was suddenly afraid, up there alone among the branches, unable to move or to call out. If only her teacher were here!

The leaves of the tree stirred suddenly, violently, as they do before a storm, and a strong gust of wind nearly blew Helen from her perch in the fork of the tree. She clung to the branch while the tree swayed to and fro in the high wind and the twigs snapped and fell about her. If only Anne would come! Then just as she was thinking that she and the tree must come tumbling down together she felt a strong hand seizing hers and Anne was helping her down to the safe earth beneath. Oh the joy of feeling it firm under her feet and Anne's reassuring hand holding hers tightly as they raced home together just before the storm broke!

After that Helen was afraid to do any more tree climbing—until one lovely spring morning the old urge came back with the scent of the mimosa tree in full bloom. She was playing in the summer house when the sweet scent came drifting in and at once she was feeling her way along the hedge to the end of the garden where the mimosa tree stood. She touched its graceful branches laden with the lovely scented blossom which came sweeping down to the grass. How beautiful it was, and how she longed to be up in the branches again, burying her face in the scent of the blossom.

For a moment she stood uncertainly, her hand on the tree trunk. Then she began to climb, feeling her way from branch to branch till she came to the little seat in the branches which she knew. She had conquered her fear. It was wonderful to be up in a tree again, best of all this mimosa with the sun shining warm on the blossom.

*　　*　　*

As her knowledge of things grew, so Helen's store of words increased. From the moment she woke in the morning she began to spell and she went on all day long. When Anne was too busy to talk to her she spelt into her own hand and carried on long conversations with herself. Now that she had found an exciting new outlet for her pent-up energy there was no stopping her in her headlong race to learn. It was like Niagara let loose!

With the key to language in her hand, Helen was determined to use it. One day she surprised Anne by asking: "What is love? Is it the scent of flowers? Or is it the warm sun?"

It was her first question about abstract things which she could not touch with her hands. She was still puzzling over Anne's answer which was not at all clear to her, when she began stringing beads in order of their size. She kept making mistakes and as she tried to rearrange the beads in the right order Anne Sullivan touched her forehead and spelled with a great deal of emphasis the word "think".

Somehow Helen knew in a flash that the word described the process that was going on in her head. It was the first time she had understood an abstract idea. That made it easier for her teacher to talk to her about love and how it shows itself.

And all the time Helen was learning to understand most about love by "seeing" and feeling it in

28

action, especially in Anne's devotion in teaching her. The closed door with which her deafness and blindness had shut her out from the world of people and things had begun to open for her because love had lifted the latch.

That was why the first Christmas, nine months after Anne came to Tuscumbia, was the happiest time Helen had ever known. She could feel love and joy in the air, in the excitement of planning with Anne gifts and surprises to make it a happy time for other people. She was invited to the school-children's party where she enjoyed her first Christmas tree. She was first made to feel the shape of the presents hanging on the branches, then to her joy Anne told her that she was to hand them round to all the children. There were a number of presents for Helen herself, and Anne was secretly pleased and proud to see that when Helen found one little girl with fewer presents than the rest she insisted on sharing hers. How different from the Helen of only a few months ago who always wanted to grab everything for herself!

On Christmas morning when the family came down to breakfast and Helen was all agog with excitement over her first Christmas stocking and all the rest of the festivities, everyone was overjoyed to see the difference in her which Anne's coming had made.

"I thank God every day of my life for sending you to us," Mrs. Keller said. "I never quite realized until this morning all that you have done for Helen—and for us."

It was a day Helen herself was always to remember—the day she had her first glimpse of understanding that

"Love was born at Christmas."

3

WIDER STILL

THE door which had kept Helen shut in the dark opened wider still as she learned to read and write.

In teaching her to read Anne helped her first with printed words in raised letters on slips of cardboard. Helen soon learned to form the words into sentences. One day she pinned on to her pinafore the word "girl", then standing in the wardrobe she put up on the shelf the other three words, "is", "in", "wardrobe"—till Anne came and found her and they had a good laugh together.

Once she had mastered the raised letters, Anne went on to teach her to read from books printed in raised characters known as braille. They often sat up in a tree poring over a book together, pretending they were two squirrels perched up in the branches. Anne made learning fun and full of interest. Nearly all Helen's lessons were out of doors, linked with living things about her. "Everything that could hum, or buzz, or sing, or bloom, had a part in my education," she said.

Her progress was so remarkable that already people were taking a great interest in her. Anne Sullivan sent frequent reports to the head of the Perkins Institute; he thought them so unusual and important that he printed them in his annual report. Soon after, in the spring of 1888, he invited Mrs. Keller, Helen and Anne to visit the school in Boston.

So once again Helen had the excitement of the long journey from the south to the north of the United States. But this time she could enter into everything with intelligent interest as Anne Sullivan wrote in her hand a description of all she could see from the window of the train—the winding river, the hills and woods, the laughing, chattering negroes on the stations with candy and popcorn to sell. People on the train were struck by Helen's intelligence, her gay interest in everything and everybody, her concern that her doll Nancy should enjoy it all too.

From the first day that they spent at the Institute Helen was completely at home, meeting and mixing with the blind girls at the school. It was her first touch with other children who could talk with their hands as she did. Until then she had always had to speak through Anne as interpreter.

During that first long stay in Boston Helen had many excitements besides meeting with the blind children at school. One day they went by steamboat to New Plymouth to see the place where the Pilgrim Fathers had landed two and a half centuries before. For Helen it was a wonderful way of learning history. To begin with, her first sea trip was a thrill in itself; then to be able to feel with her fingers the great rock where the Pilgrims from England set foot after their journey of three thousand miles across the Atlantic in the little *Mayflower*, made the story come alive for her. She was given a little model of the Plymouth Rock and on it she could trace in raised figures the date "1620" when that new chapter began in her country's history.

Another joy for Helen when the blind school closed for the summer holidays was the time that she and Anne spent by the sea. She loved the salt tang of the air and the roar of the waves whose vibration she could feel as they broke on the shore. The sea fascinated her. What fun it was to cling to a big rock in her swim-suit while the waves sent giant sprays of water over her. She quickly made friends with the sea in spite of her first experience of losing her footing and feeling the waves rush over her head.

It was all so new to her, so exciting and such fun. And all the time she was learning through each new experience as it came.

"Helen is always ready for adventure, reaching

out for something new," said the head of the blind school. He was amazed at the progress she had made with Anne Sullivan to teach her. Never had a child who was blind, deaf and dumb learned so quickly or so much, or developed such a power of expression. It was clear that Helen was going to make her mark. Perhaps one day she would become famous.

Anne Sullivan had seen for herself that Helen had remarkable powers. But she was wisely determined that she should not be turned into an infant prodigy if she could help it. When they went back to Tuscumbia she saw to it that Helen had plenty of fun and activity at home—including a pony to ride and visits to the circus.

At her first circus Helen had the time of her life. She was allowed to feed the elephants and to climb up on the back of the largest of them; she shook the paw of a bear, under the keeper's supervision, laughed when a monkey stole her hairribbon and tried to snatch the flowers from her hat. The riders and clowns and rope-walkers let her feel their costumes, and a charioteer offered to drive her round the ring. When she got home she talked on her fingers of nothing but the circus, and Anne felt obliged to read up a great deal more about animals to answer her endless questions.

At another circus, a year later, they were standing in front of a lion's cage when he gave out a great roar. Helen felt the vibration so clearly that she tried to imitate the sound.

Anne described to her what a camel looked like as she was not allowed to touch one. A few days later she found Helen on all fours with a pillow strapped on her back to leave a hollow in the middle with a hump on either side. Having perched her doll between the humps she stood up and with long, loping strides moved round the room. Anne was much amused at this ingenious way of picturing the camel which Helen had only seen through her description.

*　　*　　*

Now that her mind was fully awake Helen showed an insatiable curiosity about everything under the sun. It was question, question, all day long.

Who made the world? Where did I come from? What is God like? When Anne did her best to answer some of these eager questions, Helen said sadly: "I am blind and deaf. That is why I cannot see God." Anne taught her the word "invisible" and explained that though none of us can see God with our eyes, He is round about us like the air we breathe, and that when our hearts are full of kindness and gentleness we see Him because then we are more like Him.

But she could tell that Helen was greatly puzzled and longing to know more. She talked to Captain and Mrs. Keller about it and they decided to ask Bishop Phillips Brooks, for whom they had a great respect, if he would come and teach Helen about the Christian faith.

"Please tell me something you know about God. May I read the Book called the Bible?" she wrote on her tablet when the Bishop promised to come and help her.

He was a very understanding person. Helen felt through his kind, sensitive hands that he was her friend, and it was this feeling of trust and confidence that made the things that he said very real to her. As he talked she liked to feel the strong clasp of his fingers while Anne wrote in her other hand the truths that he spoke simply and naturally in answer to her questions.

"Love is everything," he said. "And if anyone asks you, or if you ask yourself, what God is, answer *God is love*. He is our Father and we are His children. That is the answer which the Bible gives."

Through his teaching and the letters he wrote to Helen, something of the joy and certainty which the Bishop felt through his own faith came like a flood of new light into her mind and heart. *Light:* it meant just that to Helen who for so long had lived in the dark. God was like Jesus, the One who went about doing good, giving sight to the blind, making the deaf hear and the dumb able to speak. God was like that.

Just as her mind opened with new understanding when the word "water" came to her with fresh meaning, so now with "love" as the key word, her spirit woke up to the wonder of the spiritual world about her. She felt the love of God her Father surrounding her like warmth and light. She was glad and free and happy.

And she was full of interest in other people. Bishop Brooks taught her to think of God's love as a circle which kept nobody out and wanted to draw everyone in. She told him how once when she was out with her teacher and her negro nurse, Anne would not accept ice cream because the shop refused to serve the negro girl who was with them. What did he think about that?

Bishop Brooks took her hand in his kind, strong one, then he wrote in finger language: "Because God is our loving Father we are *all* His children. He wants us to behave to one another as members of one family. We must never shut anyone out of things because the colour of his skin happens to be different from ours."

Helen never forgot that. It was all part of the new warmth and light of the Christian faith which Bishop Brooks made so real to her. Years later she wrote: "If your faith burns strong and bright, others will light their candle at it." At the age of ten she had lighted her candle from Bishop Brooks's firm faith and it was to be a light to guide her all through her life; the glowing heart of all her service for others.

4

HELEN STEPS OUT

FROM the time she was ten many exciting things began to happen to Helen Keller. Not only did her old friend, Bishop Brooks, help her to find the way into the shining Kingdom of God's love. She felt on tiptoe with a new sense of adventure because her mind as well as her spirit was now wide awake. She was bursting with life and energy and longed to express herself like everybody else.

"Why can't I talk like other people instead of with my fingers?" was a question she kept on asking.

But no one, not even Anne, thought it was possible for her ever to learn to speak because, being blind, she could not watch the lips of others, and being deaf she could not hear them speak. Still Helen would not take no for an answer and begged that a way should be found.

Then one day a friend came to see them with wonderful news. She told Helen of a deaf and blind Norwegian girl who had been taught to speak and to understand her teacher by touching her lips with her fingers.

That settled it. Helen was sure she could learn to speak too. So it was arranged that Anne should take her to a school for the deaf in Boston where the head teacher would give her a course of lessons.

*   *   *

It was hard, uphill work, with much drudgery, but Helen was so keen and determined that she struggled on. In stammering syllables she spoke her first connected sentence: "It is warm." Though at first it was not easy to understand her, her success in beginning to talk at all was far greater than anyone expected.

"Now," she said to herself in triumph, "Mildred will be able to understand me, and I shall be able to talk to Mother like anybody else."

Once she found that she really could talk to people, it meant practice, practice, practice. By placing her fingers on the lips, nose and throat of the person who was talking to her, she could tell what they were saying. Now she felt nearer to people than ever before, and that made her world so much larger. To know she could do many things now like other people spurred her on to still greater efforts.

"Helen with her blind eyes and deaf ears is seeing and hearing much more than most normal people," thought Anne Sullivan. "She'll never be daunted by obstacles." Where would it all lead to, she wondered? It was exciting to begin to look ahead. She believed that Helen with her keen interest in people and her longing for action and adventure would find a special way of helping others in the days ahead.

But the long, hard struggle of patience and perseverance had to come first. Helen and her teacher were like two explorers making their way along an unknown track in face of tremendous obstacles. With pluck and determination and sheer hard work, combined with a flash of genius, they had hit the trail that was leading Helen out of her dark and lonely existence into the everyday world of people and books and useful activity.

Anne's one thought all along was that Helen should grow up as a normal human being. She treated her as though she could see and hear and would not allow anyone to pity her. She refused to spoil or fuss over her and only praised her work when it was as good as the best that other girls and boys of her age could achieve. This made her a natural and easy companion. "Helen is a sport," other children would say when she romped with them at games, dived and swam under water, or, on those lovely winter holidays in the north, tobogganed down the steepest slopes with the best of them. She looked the picture of health with her glowing cheeks and pretty chestnut hair, her vigorous movements and her eager interest in everything that was going on.

Indoors and out, her quick mind was always on the move. Her passion for reading had grown with her visits every winter to the blind school in Boston where Mr. Anagnos, the head, kept a watchful eye on her extraordinary progress.

"Her story is as fascinating as a fairy-tale," he said to Anne. "There is something in her that attracts everyone. She is so alive and so interested in everybody and everything. I believe she is going to be an instrument of great good in the world."

He allowed Helen to spend part of each day in the library and to take down from the shelves any books she liked. She felt her way among these treasures with what she called her hungry finger tips, for the books were printed specially for the blind in the raised letters known as braille.

Her first story book was *Little Lord Fauntleroy*. Then she went on to explore *The Arabian Nights* and *Robinson Crusoe*, Hawthorne's *Wonder Book* and Dickens's *Child's History of England*; Bible stories and the *Pilgrim's Progress*, Lamb's *Tales from Shakespeare* and *The Jungle Book*—a glorious medley which opened up a new world to her. She loved *Little Women* because it made her feel close to girls and boys who could see and hear. Another favourite was a book of Greek heroes. There was something about ancient Greece which fascinated her.

One day she was sitting in the library deep in a book about Greece.

"Isn't it a strange thing," she said suddenly to Anne, "I have been such a long way away, and yet I have never left this room."

"How do you mean?" asked Anne.

"Why, I have actually been in Athens," said Helen. She had been so lost in her book that she felt she really had been living in the great Greek city of which she had been reading. The thought suddenly struck her that with her mind she could travel all over the world, like anyone else, and the wonder of it made her feel more alive than ever.

"Even if I can't see like other people," she said to Anne, "I can imagine all these other countries and people and see them with my mind's eye."

Anne was thrilled to see the way her thoughts were now turning away from herself to other people —out into the wide world teeming with interest.

"One day I shall *really* travel," announced Helen firmly.

"Perhaps you will," said Anne, secretly thinking it would not surprise her.

*   *   *

When Helen was nearly thirteen, something

happened which opened her mind still wider to the wonder of the world about her.

In the spring of 1893 she and Anne went for a holiday in the north. In Washington they saw a great deal of Helen's old friend, the famous Dr. Bell. He had taken a special interest in her ever since she first went to see him about her deafness when she was only six. Together they planned an expedition to see one of the world's wonders, the Niagara Falls.

As she stood in the presence of Niagara Helen felt overawed. She could scarcely believe it was water that she felt rushing and plunging at her feet. Though she could neither see nor hear she could feel the air vibrate and the earth tremble with the roar of the water and she was awed by the grandeur of this vast force. They went down in a lift to be near the eddies and whirlpools in the deep gorge below the Falls, and went over the wonderful suspension bridge which crosses the gorge at a great height above the water. As she stood there in the presence of so much grandeur Helen little knew that an English traveller was to remark before long: "The United States possesses two of the world's wonders—Helen Keller and the Falls of Niagara."

Her experience that day of so great a marvel of Nature was something to remember. So too was her visit soon after to the World's Fair in Chicago, where she saw some of the wonders of science, art and industry. For three exciting weeks, with Dr. Bell to explain to her the chief exhibits, she revelled in the novelty of the Fair. To Helen it felt like one long voyage of discovery as day after day she took in fresh wonders through her finger-tips. For as a special privilege the president of the Fair gave her permission to touch the exhibits and to hold some of them in her hands. She recognized the India of her books in the curios she handled in the eastern bazaar. The land of Egypt came alive as with her fingers she felt a model Cairo and picked out the mosques and the long processions of camels. Another time she went aboard a Viking ship, but best of all, she thought, was the model of the *Santa Maria* in which Columbus sailed. The captain showed her Columbus's cabin and the desk with the hour-glass which the great discoverer would have used.

Everything fascinated Helen—whether it was things of beauty like the French and the Japanese bronzes, so life-like to her touch, or marvels of invention like the telephone which Dr. Bell let her hold while he explained in her other hand how it worked—how one human voice could speak to another at a distance.

In those three weeks at the Fair Helen began to grow up. She had come in touch with real life and she found it even more exciting than the fairy stories of her childhood. Through the exhibits she had in imagination made a trip round the world. And as she felt with her fingers the marvels of man's invention, his industry and skill, she woke up to the interest and importance of the workaday world close at hand.

★   ★   ★

After the Fair was over a friend sent Helen a souvenir. It was a little shield to remind her of Columbus and to suggest that she was making discoveries too. Helen wondered at first what this meant. "Do please explain why I am a discoverer," she wrote back.

She little knew how her fame as a "discoverer" was spreading. No one blind and deaf had made such discoveries before of how to lead a happy, normal life. People both in America and in Europe were following her progress with the greatest interest and admiration. Mr. Anagnos at the blind school spoke of her as the "eighth wonder of the world", and spread news of her achievements on his visits to Europe. He read one of Helen's lively letters to the Queen of Greece, and her name was already well known to Queen Victoria who asked news of her from Bishop Phillips Brooks when he was presented in London.

In America, many leading people in the world of art and literature made a point of getting to know her. After Dr. Bell, one of Helen's best friends was the humorous author, Mark Twain, whom she met at a party. He told his friends that to his mind the most interesting characters of the nineteenth century were Napoleon—and Helen Keller!

Anne Sullivan was very sensible in the way she looked after Helen and kept her from being spoilt through being in the limelight. She knew it was good for her to meet all kinds of people, for if she grew up just to be a bookworm, what use would she be in the world? Helen was not the least timid or shy. Authors and actors, painters and poets, statesmen and politicians were among the many she met in her early teens. Her easy contacts with such people who in their turn felt the better and the braver for having known this gay, adventurous blind and deaf girl, were one of the most remarkable signs of Helen's growth. No wonder they thought she was like Columbus in discovering a new world. She was in fact opening up a new world of hope for other blind-deaf people like herself—but who, unlike her, had had no Anne Sullivan to rescue them from silence and the dark.

5

THE ADVENTURE BEGINS

ONCE Helen had begun to conquer her dark-ness her one thought was how she could be of some use in the world. God's love had reached down to her in the dark through strong and wise Anne Sullivan. Now she longed to be just such a strong hand to others who could neither see nor hear. That longing set her off on a great adventure.

It all began with Tommy Stringer. From the moment she heard of him her fellow feeling went rushing out in an effort to help. For Tommy had become blind and deaf and dumb when he was four. His mother had died and as his father was too poor to look after him, the child had been sent to an almshouse.

"If *only* he could go to the blind school in Boston!" exclaimed Helen. "Then he could be taught and he would have fun and be happy again."

"Yes," agreed Anne, "but that would need money and Tommy's father is too poor even to look after him at home."

"Somehow we'll raise it," said Helen promptly.

And she meant it. Anne could always tell when she was set on getting something done. She would move mountains if they were in her way. Nothing should be allowed to hold up Tommy's education. She was sure God wanted Tommy to be taught; He would show her how she could help.

He did—by turning her first real sorrow into an unexpected way of getting people interested in Tommy Stringer. It happened like this.

When her lovely dog Lioness was killed in an accident, Helen was heart-broken. She had loved her faithful dog so dearly and it was like losing a friend. To show their sympathy her friends began to raise money to buy her another dog. Helen thought how kind they were, and then the idea suddenly came to her: "Suppose this money could help to send Tommy to school!"

With her passion for writing letters (and very good ones too), she wrote round to her friends asking them if she could use their gifts in this way instead. She and Anne were having Tommy to stay with them in the spring. Helen said in her letters how happy she was to think that by the next spring this helpless and lonely small boy might be enjoying school and finding there the light and happiness that had come to her through being taught.

As the news spread of how Helen wanted to spend the money, people's imagination was stirred. Gifts came pouring in from many parts of America and from England too. Her old friends, Bishop Brooks and Dr. Bell, encouraged her, and the English painter, Millais, sent a contribution to the fund. Helen's letters to the newspapers brought many generous gifts in reply. Before long there was enough money in the fund to provide for Tommy's education. At five he was admitted to the kindergarten at the blind school in Boston—in the spring of the year just as Helen had hoped.

She was thrilled. It was her first experience of what money could do when it was turned into an active way of helping people. And at the end of Tommy's first term at school it was exciting to hear how he was getting on—even though to start with he showed much more capacity for getting into mischief than for learning to spell!

The next thing Helen thought of was to give a big tea party to raise money for the blind. In writing to her friend, Mark Twain, to ask for his help she said that all who came to her tea party would be "buying light"—the light of knowledge and love for children who were blind and friendless. She remembered so well, she wrote, what it felt like to live in the dark before her teacher came: "Then I was like the little blind children who are waiting to enter the kindergarten. There was no light in my soul. This wonderful world with all its sunlight and beauty was hidden from me, and I had never dreamed of its loveliness. But my teacher came to me and taught my fingers to use the key that has unlocked the door of my dark prison and set my spirit free."

Mark Twain gladly came to her help and the tea was a great success. It was held in the large house of a generous friend, and brought in more than two thousand dollars for the blind children.

Helen had started something bigger than she knew. She had won the interest of numbers of people in work for the blind—and she had tasted the joy of planning and carrying through practical ways of serving those whose need she specially understood and cared about.

But she never did anything by half measures. She wanted the best for those she longed to help and she knew she had a long way to go yet in getting the training she needed to fit her for the work she was to do in the world.

*　　*　　*

It was like the bursting of a bomb among her family and friends when one day she announced firmly: "I want to go to college." She guessed what their instant reaction would be and hurried on to explain: "Then when I get a degree I shall have proved that a blind and deaf person can be just as well educated as anyone else. And the better educated I am, the better fitted I shall be for the work I want to do."

People were incredulous and tried to put her off for they were sure she was doomed to disappointment. "Why, such a thing has never been done before!" was the stock objection. "No blind and deaf person has ever gone to college." It was quite the wrong argument to convince Helen. The fact that it had never been done before was an added reason for attempting it.

"But do stop and think, Helen," said one well-meaning but unadventurous friend. "Even to pass the entrance exams you'll need German and French and Latin as well as English, and Greek and Roman history too. And then suppose you did manage to get as far as that, you could never hope to go right through a college course. You can't hear lectures, you can't make notes, and you have no books. What *is* the use of attempting something in which you are bound to fail?"

Such friends thought they were being so helpful and practical but for Helen they had left out of count the most important fact of all. They had forgotten God and His purpose—and His power.

Only Anne stood by her in the decision she had made—brave, adventurous Anne who had such faith that Helen could and would succeed in this great venture. All along she had treated Helen as an ordinary human being and so helped her to take her place among other girls. For Anne firmly refused to think of blind people as a class apart.

So with her help and encouragement Helen went ahead with her studies to prepare for college. The head of the girls' school where she attended classes for a time in preparation said she seemed to look upon difficulties as merely "new heights to be scaled". By the time she was nineteen she had passed her examinations and could have gone to college straightaway. But knowing she would have a struggle to work as quickly as the others she spent another year studying hard with a private teacher. Then in the year 1900 she entered Radcliffe College. It was the moment she had looked forward to for years. She entered on equal terms with the rest, embarking on the full college course like any other student. Helen neither asked for nor was given any special favours or concessions. She knew the college authorities did not really want her there at all, but that only made her more determined than ever to succeed.

Thrilled as she was to have actually entered college, the obstacles were enough to daunt the most adventurous pioneer. To begin with, there was the great difficulty over books. At that time few books had been printed for the blind and Helen had to have many expensive text-books copied for her in braille, or borrowed for her use from England and Germany. She had to have a specially made typewriter for her written work, and a machine for "embossing" algebra. This was all very costly and was only made possible by the help of her friends, especially Mark Twain; together they raised a fund to pay her way through college. For by this time Helen's father had died and her family was unable to support her in the heavy extra expense of her education.

Then there was the great difficulty of keeping up with the lectures. Anne sat beside her in class, rapidly spelling the day's lectures into her hand. Anne herself strained her weak sight in reading to Helen books on philosophy, history and economics, and in looking up words for her in Latin, German and French—even though she did not understand these languages herself. What faith they both needed to persevere in face of such obstacles! Helen revelled in books and study, but her blindness and deafness made everything take so much longer, and the tedious methods she had to use turned much of her work into drudgery. At times she felt overwhelmed. She was such a gay, friendly person and her handicaps often made her feel lonely and isolated from other people. She longed to join in the social life of the college, but her studies under such difficulties left her with little opportunity, for she and Anne had to work far into the night to keep up. Helen would come back from an occasional tramp with the other girls, or from the glorious freedom of a toboggan run on a winter's evening, and then have to settle down to the hard grind of study without sight to help her. Feeling rebellious and exasperated she would try to steady her mind by thinking of people of courage and tenacity like Joan of Arc and Christopher Columbus, of ancient heroes like Socrates and Ulysses. Always in the worst moments she found fresh courage in what she called "the faith that turns my darkness into light". There would come to steady her spirit a sure sense of the loving presence of God about her, making her brave to go on.

That was how she won through. She had entered Radcliffe when she was twenty, and four years later she graduated with honours. She left the university with the unique distinction of being the first blind and deaf person ever to go through college. The newspapers published the news of her success, and her beautifully typed examination papers have been preserved in the Harvard Museum—a striking answer to the objections made to her competing for a degree. Helen Keller had proved to the world that it was possible for the doubly handicapped to develop as well as anyone else. She was blazing a new trail for others to follow.

6

CRUSADE AGAINST DARKNESS

AFTER her strenuous years at college, Helen was ready for a break. This gave her time to enjoy the new adventure of home-making. For she and Anne Sullivan were now able to set up house together on their own.

Helen had always loved her father's farm in the sunny south, with all the animals and livestock as well as the old house with its orchard and garden. As she grew up she longed to live on a farm again. Now the chance had come. With some money given to them by a friend she and Anne bought a small old farmhouse in the village of Wrentham, outside Boston. Though the house was very neglected they were able, with a few alterations, to make it attractive and homelike. There was a garden, and a big field of seven acres where Helen's dog Phiz could have a run. There was also a pine wood near by, and a lake where they could swim.

To Helen one of the joys of the new home at Wrentham was that she could have a study of her own. This was made out of what had previously been two pantries and the dairy room. On the wall she hung one of her special treasures—a bas-relief medallion of the blind poet, Homer. With her fingers she could trace the features of that fine, sad face, and she took courage from the thought of all he gave to the world through his blindness. On shelves round the room she arranged her braille library of Greek and Latin, French and German books and her favourite English and American poets.

The big east window was full of plants that she loved to look after. The study also had a glass door which led out into a cluster of pine trees where she could sit and think out what she wanted to write. For writing, she found, was a wonderful way of getting in touch with people near and far and winning their sympathy for work among the blind. She had always been good at letter-writing, and at college she had written a number of articles which had been published. She had also been encouraged to write the story of her own experiences. This she made into a book with the help of John Macy, a Harvard graduate who was a literary critic and journalist, and a great friend of Anne's. He learned the hand alphabet in order to talk to Helen and help her complete her manuscript.

The book was published in 1904, the year she left college. The story of her life told thus in her own words, with her obvious gift for writing, was soon to make Helen Keller famous. It proved so popular that in time it appeared in fifty different languages as well as being printed in braille for the blind.

★   ★   ★

In all the help he gave Helen with her writing and through his friendship with Anne, John Macy became almost part of the household at Wrentham. It had been obvious for some time that he was greatly attracted by handsome, distinguished Anne Sullivan. Now much to Helen's joy they were to be married and John was to come and live with them at the farmhouse.

Shortly before the wedding Helen received a mysterious letter which said on the outside "a secret for Helen Keller". Underneath was written: "I don't want Miss Sullivan or Mr. Macy to read this note. Let someone else read it to Helen."

She took it to a friend who was staying with them and asked her to read it. It was a letter from Dr. Bell asking her to buy Anne a wedding present from him with the cheque he enclosed; Anne herself was not to know anything about it until Helen had chosen the present. So she and the friend went off to Boston to choose something specially nice for Dr. Bell to give Anne. After a long search

Helen decided on two presents—a clock with a soft chime and a silver coffee urn.

Helen liked John Macy. He was witty and very good company. After he and Anne were married and he joined them at the farmhouse they had good times together, for all three had much in common, especially their love of books.

John's work took him to Boston every day. While Anne drove him to the station first thing in the morning and then did the shopping, Helen cleared the breakfast table, washed the dishes and tidied the rooms. Then she and Anne would set to work on their letters. Their mail grew thick and fast as more and more people realized how much these two could give to blind and handicapped people, out of their own experience.

In the evenings when John Macy came home, they read and talked and discussed plans together. Helen was full of ideas now that she knew what her work in the world was to be. Her one fear had always been that her great handicaps would prevent her from taking an active share in things and would make her a useless member of society. Now she knew that God was calling her to use her own strange experience to give courage to others afflicted like herself but without her advantages. He could use her to help those who were living in the dark without a faith to light up the way.

"I would love to help both the blind *and* the

deaf," she said, "but as I can't do both, I shall do all I can for the blind. I want to help those who've lost their work and can't support themselves—I know just how helpless they must feel."

She had already linked up with a pioneer group in Boston who wanted to help the blind to help themselves and to live as normal a life as possible. The group knew that their first step must be to persuade the Government to back their efforts, so Helen Keller was asked to go with a deputation to win State support.

It was a great moment for her when she had to appear before the State authorities to plead the cause of the blind. When the Government agreed to appoint a Commission to discover ways of providing work for blind people so that they could earn a living, Helen felt that her life work had really begun.

"The blind see with their hands," she said. Those hands must be trained to make useful saleable goods, not the silly, trifling things which were often thought of as suitable for handicapped people to make. Why should they not become clever at such skills as carpentry and wood-work, weaving and chair-making, massage and piano-tuning?

The idea caught on. Trades were taught to the blind in their homes and an attractive shop was opened in a fashionable shopping centre in Boston to sell the things they made. Soon the new Commission was able to open a series of shops in different parts of the State of Massachusetts. People found that these shops were worth going to for everything was well made and of practical use—hand-woven curtains and table covers, bedspreads and rugs and linen suits, all of good design and finish. It was a display which showed how well the blind could be trained to make useful things to sell at a fair price. And what a difference it made to the blind craftsmen to realize that they belonged not only to the brotherhood of the blind, but to the great human brotherhood of the world's workers!

"Now they have worth-while work to do they feel they're some use in the world," said Helen Keller who knew so well what it felt like.

Another way in which she fought her crusade against darkness was to make it easier for the blind to read books. At present each state had its own way of printing books for the blind. As Helen knew to her cost there were as many as five different kinds of print used in America; she had had to learn to read in them all. It was most confusing for it meant that a blind person taught to read in one state could not read the books printed in another state.

"Oh dear," exclaimed Helen, "what a lot of wasted effort there is because each state works on its own with no idea of what the others are doing! If only we could all pull together what a difference it would make!"

She set herself to work for the day when all books for the blind should be printed in one style only—the method of raised dots known as braille. It took her a long time to win this battle of the books, but she persevered and at last her idea of having them all printed in one style won the day. Today braille is used by the blind everywhere.

*   *   *

In the midst of all her work for the blind Helen Keller had the feeling that she was still not giving the very best that she might.

"If I am to be a real spokesman for the blind," she said, "I *must* be able to speak better. People are very kind but I know they can't understand half the time what I say."

It was true. People were fascinated by her story but found her voice difficult to listen to; it was very monotonous and her words were indistinct. She determined to practise and practise until she could do better.

"If *only* I could hear myself what my voice sounds like!" she would say to Anne after she had tried and tried to follow her teacher's suggestions for getting more expression into her voice. Anne wrote rapidly into her hand of the rippling movement of a brook and the full-throated song of a bird, and again Helen would try to speak with expression and form her words more clearly.

This was one of the hardest battles she had to fight. Often she was so discouraged by her failures to speak normally that it was only with a tremendous effort of will that she went on in the hope of succeeding.

Yet already she had advanced a very long way. She could look back to the time she was ten, when as she said, "my thoughts used to beat against my finger-tips like birds striving to gain their freedom." Then the door opened as she was taught to utter her first stumbling words, and after the eleventh lesson she had gone home repeating that wonderful sentence, "I-am-not-dumb-any-more." Gradually her "speech-wings" had begun to get stronger with practice and use. Now they longed to soar. Already she could speak better than many deaf people, but she was sure God wanted her to improve still more and that with His help she could learn to use her voice as He intended.

She worked away at it with all her energy and determination. A well-known teacher of singing in Boston became so interested in her efforts to use her voice more naturally that he offered to give her lessons. He learned the hand alphabet so that he could teach her just like any other pupil.

He gave her endless encouragement and she needed every bit of it. For often her voice seemed quite unmanageable. One moment it would be a high-pitched falsetto, the next it would dive down low. Often it seemed as though she never could learn to speak like other people.

"Oh, it's *too* difficult!" she exclaimed in despair. But she still went on. In the end it meant more than three years of patient hard work before her singing master thought Helen's voice was sufficiently improved for her to make a public appearance. In February 1913 it was arranged that she and Anne should give a demonstration at a town in New Jersey. Anne would explain how she had taught her blind and deaf pupil to use her mind and to live a practically normal life. Helen was to show how she had overcome her difficulty in speaking.

When the day came she was so strung up with all the effort and longing to do well that she was overcome with fright. As she went on to the platform she prayed desperately: "O God, please let me pour out my voice freely." Then standing there before the crowd of interested, excited people she felt frozen with terror and her heart seemed to stop beating. She opened her lips but no sound came though the words were longing to tumble out. At last she made a sound which felt to her like a cannon going off though to the audience it was only a whisper. Then summoning all her pluck and will power she made a start and somehow struggled through the speech she had prepared, though her voice was very uncertain and indistinct.

She knew she had done badly and as soon as the meeting was over she hurried from the platform feeling utterly miserable. Of course everyone was specially kind to her and tried to cheer and encourage her. But she knew she had failed. She had so longed to help the cause of the handicapped by showing how such difficulties could be overcome, and now she felt she had failed them.

Yet that failure proved one of her finest moments after all. She refused to be beaten by it. Instead it toughened her spiritual muscles and made her stronger in God's service. "In a little while (she wrote later) faith and hope and love came back and I returned to my practising." Gradually she gained more confidence and learned to speak much better. People flocked to hear her and greatly admired her courage in dealing with her handicaps.

It was a wonderful story she had to tell, and she always looked so attractive and full of life that it did people good to see her. She was a tall, erect figure with a fine shaped head and good features, and she dressed well for she had a great love of beauty and enjoyed the feel of good clothes. Besides, as an ambassador of the blind she wanted to look her best for their sake. She disliked dullness and drabness and thought it out of place in a world God meant to be beautiful. In her addresses she often spoke of our duty to be happy, and her audience thought how well she practised what she preached.

"Blind people have just the same right to be happy too," she said. "But this can never be unless they are trained for some work by which they can support themselves. Think what it must feel like to live on charity and to feel yourself a burden to others."

Then as she described some of the sightless people she knew who had been taught various industries and were now able to make useful things for sale, her audience realized what a wonderful work it was to which she was giving her life and was now asking for their help.

* * *

Her crusade against darkness was leading Helen Keller to many new discoveries.

Though she had lived a sheltered life in the country until she grew up, she was now making it her business to find out how other people lived in the big industrial towns and cities. Even as a child she had gone with Anne and Dr. Bell into the slums of New York, and now as she travelled about she came to know a great deal of the wretched, sordid conditions of life in the back alleys of the industrial cities, where people lived in great ugly tenements and the children grew up underfed and in rags. Without actually seeing it she could feel and smell poverty and squalor, and with her quick imagination she knew what it must be like to live in such misery and want.

"But it's no use just being sorry for people," she said. She used her knowledge to work for the improvement of conditions in which the poor lived. By fighting for changes in living conditions in the big cities she was also fighting the cause of the blind. For she knew that such evils as poverty and ignorance are often the real cause of much blindness.

She was both angry and grieved at any kind of injustice or oppression, but she never grew bitter. She was too fine a Christian for that. She owed it to her old friend Bishop Brooks that she had learned to fight with the right weapons; to be so sure of God as a loving Father, wanting the best for all His children, that her chief aim was to forward His work in the world and to try to do it in His way. "Love is the greatest thing in the world," she remembered he had said, "and God is love." Her faith was a torch shining in the dark, whether it was the physical darkness in which the blind had to live, or the spiritual darkness of those without the knowledge of God's love and care.

It was this faith which armed her in her crusade against both kinds of darkness.

7

CRUSADER ON WHEELS

"ONE day I shall travel," Helen Keller had said when she was twelve and her mind was waking up to the fact of other peoples and places to be explored. Now her work for the blind was taking her to many cities and towns on the eastern side of America.

But before her journeys gave her any real enjoyment there was much she had to get used to because of her blindness and deafness. It was not easy to leave the homely, familiar surroundings at Wrentham in which she knew her way about, and to plunge into the whirl of city life without being able to see what was going on around her. She often thought longingly of the peaceful garden at home, of the walk she could do alone to the pine wood because John Macy had fixed up a wire along the edge of the field where she could feel her way. Now in all the thronging, jostling life of a big city she often felt lonely and isolated for she depended entirely on Anne or another friend who had joined them in the work, to write in her hand a description of all that was going on about her.

Never did she feel more lonely or afraid than during the trip when she and Anne were due to give a lecture together in one of the big cities. In the strange hotel where they spent the night Anne woke up in the morning feeling ill with a sudden attack of influenza. Helen was in a panic. What could she do? She never felt at home in hotels at the best of times and now her helplessness swept over her afresh for she could neither use the telephone nor find her way downstairs alone. At last help came, a doctor was sent for, and the manager of the hotel eventually saw them safely on to a train home.

But in spite of all the difficulties Helen was always eager for adventure. "Life is either a daring adventure or nothing," she would say, and gradually she grew more accustomed to moving about the country by train, car and taxi—a crusader on wheels. For now that the idea of training blind workers in all kinds of industries was beginning to take hold, the next step was to visit as many towns and cities as possible to bring home to people their responsibility to support this work for the blind.

She and Anne went everywhere together. They made a striking pair when they appeared on a public platform to speak and answer questions, and the welcome they were always given cheered and encouraged them. Anne was a naturally good speaker, and people listened with tremendous interest while she explained first how she had taught Helen. Then when it was Helen's turn to demonstrate their method of working together, she would place her fingers on Anne's mouth and show that she could read her lips while she talked, and when Anne wrote into her hand she could tell the audience what she said in that way too.

*   *   *

In 1914 they set off on their longest journey yet —right across the American continent. This time, much to Helen's joy, her mother went too and she was able to make things much easier for them both by buying their railway tickets, booking their hotel rooms, looking after the shopping, and dealing with visitors. Mrs. Keller had always longed to travel and now they could all three enjoy this first long journey together.

What a thrill it was—even though it was not always sheer enjoyment. They lectured in Canadian cities where they were given a great welcome, then back in the United States they spoke in various towns in the Middle West. Their next long hop was from Salt Lake City to Los Angeles in lovely California.

On this trip they all had a narrow escape. They left Salt Lake City in biting cold, wrapped up in fur coats, lined gloves and boots. Then one night when they were fast asleep their train jumped the rails and the violence of the movement nearly threw them out of their berths. They had to dress as fast as they could in the dark and then scramble out on to the track and continue their journey in a primitive and uncomfortable train.

Helen had no more sleep that night, but as the train rumbled on and daylight came she was suddenly aware of a lovely scent drifting in through the window. Her mother and Anne took it in turns to spell into her hand a description of the scenery they were passing through. The delicious scent on the morning air came from the orange blossom and from the sage bushes on the hills, and there were masses of bright coloured flowers too, blue, gold and scarlet. They were not far now from Los Angeles.

They had so looked forward to this moment but now after the train accident they felt very tired and travel-worn. And how unsuitably dressed they knew they must look in their fur wraps, for as the train drew in they saw gathered there on the platform in the warm sunshine a crowd of well-dressed people who had come to meet them—the women in pretty summer frocks and hats, and carrying gay parasols! As the tired travellers stepped on to the platform they were instantly surrounded by a friendly crowd and numbers of press reporters and photographers. They felt so embarrassed that they hailed a taxi as soon as they could and drove off to their hotel for a good rest and the chance to change into summer clothes.

The trip to California was one they always remembered—it was so full of sunshine and sweet scents and beautiful things to enjoy. Helen could usually tell which part of the city she was in by the particular scent which she recognized. She loved too the joy of movement, of sailing across San Francisco Bay with Anne or her mother to describe its loveliness and to tell her of the ships that came sailing into the harbour, laden with cargoes from the Far East. It made her long to sail the way those ships had come. Perhaps one day she would.

Besides the spell of the gleaming gold and blue waters of the Bay there was the wonder of the forests; of the mighty redwood trees for which California is famed. To walk through the Muir Woods and to touch with her hands the trunks of these giants of the forest made her feel as though she stood in some vast cathedral. "God seems to walk invisible through the long dim aisles," she wrote later in her book describing these travels.

That wonderful trip right across America from east to west and back again was the first of Helen Keller's far adventures and typical of many more to come. For she and Anne continued to travel all over the United States on their lecture tours for the blind. Their journeys took them from the shores of the Atlantic to the Pacific coast. Anne tried to describe to Helen as best she could the changing scene from the train window, as they sped over vast plains and prairies, or among mountains and wooded hills.

Helen grew to love this experience of covering great distances, and to enjoy the rhythmic movement of the train on a long journey. She learned to adapt herself to all kinds of odd, sometimes exasperating circumstances. She had a keen sense of humour and a tremendous interest in all that was going on around her.

Everywhere she and Anne went they spoke for the blind, of the right of every blind person to be given a chance to live a happy, useful life in the world. Sometimes they spoke in a noisy tent crowded with country folk, sometimes in churches and town halls, sometimes in mining-towns and mill-towns where they came close to the workers in industry and tried to share their problems and difficulties. Helen was so interested in people that she would go anywhere to meet them. On her travels she met all sorts and conditions. In the big cities she had the chance of meeting many famous people. They thought of her as the famous one, for no blind and deaf person had ever before succeeded in conquering their handicaps as she had done. Thomas Edison, the inventor of the gramophone, and Caruso, the great singer, were both deeply interested in this woman who had conquered her deafness to the extent of being able to enjoy music by the feel of the vibrations or by the sense of touch. Caruso sang for her while she "listened" with her fingers on his lips. She was interested in things mechanical too, and much enjoyed being taken over the great Ford motor works in Detroit by Henry Ford himself. He told her how he had first thought of the idea of building a car that the farmer could afford to buy, and then he had learned to make it. He was a very good friend to the blind and when Helen Keller met him again some years later he told her he was employing seventy-three blind men in his plants, not out of pity but because they proved efficient workers.

★   ★   ★

Much as Helen Keller enjoyed her travels they were by no means all excitement and adventure. There were dull and dreary days when everything seemed to go wrong and their work was disappointing and people were tiresome and difficult. She was exasperated at times to find how stupid people could be about the blind. She had to explain as patiently as she could how like others they are. In one of her books she describes the way she had to explain things to people with little imagination: "I tell them that blind people are like other people in the dark; that fire burns them, and cold chills them, and they like food when they are hungry, and drink when they are thirsty, and some of them like one lump of sugar in their tea, and others more!"

Fortunately her sense of humour often came to the rescue when she felt tired and irritated. She had the sense to see how unimportant were such trifles beside the really big troubles in life. By this time the shadow of the First World War was haunting everyone, and people in America were wondering whether their own country would be drawn in. Helen was much distressed about it all and found it difficult to concentrate on her work, though she did her best to carry on through the war years. She and Anne had their own personal troubles as well, especially as Anne's poor health and failing sight made it difficult for her to travel.

Besides her anxiety about Anne, Helen was very worried about money matters too. Their resources were dwindling fast with so much travelling about at their own expense, so they decided to sell their home at Wrentham and buy a smaller house. It was a great wrench to give up the old farmhouse which had been their home for thirteen years, and move into a rather ugly brick cottage in a suburb of New York City.

By this time John Macey was working more and

more away from home. Anne and Helen were glad that they now had a secretary who lived with them and shared in all the work and was a loyal friend to them both. Her name was Polly Thompson. She took over the running of the house and was the greatest help to them in all kinds of ways, especially now that Anne's health was beginning to fail. Now they could relax for a bit after their strenuous travels abroad.

8

NEW WAYS TO ONE END

THEY had only just settled down in their new home in New York when Helen received an exciting letter. A generous American who wanted to put his money to good use suggested that a film of her life story would have a great message for the world. It would also give her a means of earning a living. With high hopes they all three set out to cross the continent again, bound this time for Hollywood.

It proved an unusual adventure, with many ups and downs during the several weeks they spent there. At first Helen enjoyed the newness of it all. Every morning at sunrise she and Polly Thompson went for a ride on horseback, on the trails of Beverly Hills. One morning her horse slipped his saddle and Helen was thrown into a strawberry bed while the horse cantered off.

Another time they went for a drive out to the desert over miles of sand with an occasional cactus or shrub. Suddenly her companion wrote excitedly in Helen's hand: "I can see a real Red Indian!" They got out of the car and the men in the party approached the figure in his gorgeous headdress of eagles' feathers, meaning to ask him if Miss Keller might touch his wonderful plumage. Much to their surprise he answered their miming in perfectly good English: of course the lady could feel his headdress as much as she liked! He turned out to be a film actor waiting for his camera-men to turn up! Helen realized that with film-making all kinds of odd happenings were likely to come her way.

It was not surprising that with her great handicaps of blindness and deafness she found it hard to follow the producer's directions, all of which had to be spelled into her hand by Polly Thompson. The picture was to be called *Deliverance*. Having decided that there was not enough excitement or romance in Helen Keller's own story to make a good film, the producers invented all kinds of far-fetched adventures for her. One pictured her as the Mother of Sorrows carrying a torch of hope to the blind, the wounded and the maimed. This was one of the more successful experiments, but most of the time Helen felt wooden and awkward in front of the camera. She was sure in her own mind that she was not a real actress or film star and would never feel graceful or at ease in the various parts she was asked to play.

What appealed to her more was the work out of doors to film the background to the stories they invented for her. She enjoyed a visit to the ship-yards and the christening of a ship about to be launched. Most exciting of all was her first trip in an aeroplane. It was a small plane and there was only room for herself and the pilot. At first Anne and Mrs. Keller (who had come with them on the trip) would not hear of Helen making the flight, but she persisted and had her way. As the plane gathered speed and shot up high above the tallest building in Los Angeles, then later came down in a series of dips, she was fascinated and said she had never known such a wonderful sense of freedom before.

Another thing that specially interested Helen was the chance to meet a number of film stars, including Charlie Chaplin who learned the hand alphabet in order to talk to her. His kindness and friendliness were something she always remembered when she thought of Hollywood.

In spite of all the hard work she put into it her own film was not a success. When it failed at the box office she was disappointed but not very surprised. She began to think that it had been conceited of her to go all the way to Hollywood imagining that her story would really make a film. But she learnt much from the experience because it had shown her another side of life.

After the Hollywood adventure she and Anne were glad to enjoy their own home for a time, then

Helen became anxious because they were short of money again. So they set out on another experiment; this time they went on the stage and acted in variety. In their short act, which lasted about twenty minutes, Anne explained how she had taught Helen, then Helen spoke and after that the audience asked questions. In spite of her handicaps Helen felt close to the audience because they were so friendly, and the audience enjoyed her because she always looked so happy and they admired her pluck.

When the stage interlude was over they lived at home again and Helen worked at her voice practice and settled down to write two books which she had promised her publishers. One was the second story of her life which she called *Midstream*. It was a good description for she was now well launched on her voyage of discovery on behalf of those who like herself had to live in the dark.

*   *   *

Then came a new opportunity. The thing she had longed for happened: a national movement for the blind was started in 1921, and she and Anne were asked to help in this big effort.

"Isn't it wonderful," Helen exclaimed, "to think that at last we shall have one big movement for the whole of America instead of all the separate little

efforts in the different states!" For that was what
the rather dull-sounding name, American Foundation for the Blind, really stood for.

She saw now how all their pioneer work in the
past had prepared her for this. There were those
long tours which she and Anne had carried through
on their own and which had taught them so much.
Then acting on the stage had given her far more
confidence in using her voice, and it had made her
feel more independent to know that she could
earn her own living.

The new movement for the blind began in a
small way in New York, with private individuals
meeting the cost. But as it grew, a great deal more
money was needed to support it. An appeal must
be made to the public. Helen Keller was asked to
take a leading share in raising funds and lecturing
on behalf of the Foundation.

"If only we can make a success of it," she
thought, "here is the way to make my dream come
true of a brighter, happier world for the blind!"

How she prayed and planned and worked for it!
For the next three years she and Anne toured the
States from coast to coast and addressed thousands and thousands of people in well over a hun-
dred cities.

What a response they had! Gifts came pouring
in from all over the country. Millionaires con-
tributed many thousands of dollars. The President

of the United States in receiving Helen Keller at the White House offered his help and a generous gift, and wealthy friends of hers in Washington helped to swell the fund. Letters poured in from people in all walks of life, many with slender means—old soldiers, deaf and blind people, hundreds of children—all enclosing gifts for the Foundation. Some of the children's gifts touched her most: they would come and empty their savings in her lap, and one small invalid boy "said it with flowers" as well as a big gift of money.

It cheered Helen tremendously and helped her to give her best in the speeches she made for the blind. She was now a national figure, appealing for a national cause. People thought her such a wonderful example of what could be done to help the blind to live a full and happy life like other people, that she herself was the best possible advertisement for the cause.

Her work was not all plain sailing of course. As they toured the country she found how much stupid prejudice had to be overcome. Many still looked down on the blind and thought of them more as objects of charity than people needing a square deal and the chance to live a useful, active life. How she had to fight again and again this idea of *pitying* the blind instead of doing something practical to help them to stand on their own feet!

83

"Thank goodness Anne would never allow people to pity me," she thought. All that she owed to Anne was so much in Helen's mind that she loved to have the chance of telling people about her. In all the travelling, lecturing and writing of these tremendously busy years it was their wonderful partnership that she liked to dwell on. She knew, and said so, that without Anne Macy, Helen Keller would never have arrived.

★　　　★　　　★

It worried her to see that Anne was no longer well and strong and that her sight was failing rapidly though she still went gamely on.

"We'll all go abroad for a holiday and enjoy ourselves," said Helen. So in the spring of 1930, when Anne was recovering from a serious operation, they left America for the first time to spend a holiday in Britain. What an excitement it was for Helen! Even when the ship ran into a storm in mid-Atlantic she did not mind; it was all part of the adventure of visiting a new country.

As they drove through the streets of Plymouth in bright sunshine she was thrilled to think that from here some of her ancestors had set sail two and a half centuries before, leaving the Old World for the New. In the streets they passed carts laden with spring flowers whose scent brought home to Helen something of the beauty of an English

spring. Anne wrote rapidly into her hand a running commentary on the lovely countryside
through which they drove, so that Helen with her
vivid imagination could make her own picture of
the river sparkling in the sun, the violets in drifts
of blue, the thatched cottages and the old stone
churches. Then after they had passed from Devon
into Cornwall, and the car began to climb steeply,
what joy it was to be told that up there, high on a
cliff round which the white gulls flashed and
dived, stood the bungalow where they were to
stay for some weeks.

Helen was thankful for this carefree holiday in
Britain before returning to a whirl of activity in
America, for the Foundation.

"Another dream coming true," she said to
Anne, as she plunged into her work again. "Just
think of it—a conference now for blind people
from all over the world, not just from America.
What a glorious adventure!"

She thought of all the people who would soon
be on their way to New York for this first *world*
conference for the blind. Delegates, with their
guides and interpreters, would be coming from
China and Japan, Australia and New Zealand,
from India, South Africa, Egypt, Uruguay, and
most of Europe. As she set to work to prepare the
speech of welcome she had been asked to make to
all the visitors when they arrived, she felt this was

one of the most thrilling things that had happened to her. Not only had she been asked to make the speech of welcome—she was to go on to Washington with the delegates to present them to the President of the United States.

Helen Keller was becoming an international figure, known and respected throughout the world as a champion of the blind.

9

STILL OUTWARD BOUND

AT the height of her fame as a champion of the blind Helen Keller met with the greatest test in her life. She was left to carry on her work alone, without Anne.

During Anne's last illness a well-meaning friend had said: "Teacher, you *must* get well. Without you, Helen would be nothing."

Anne shook her head sadly. "But that would mean that I have failed," she said. And she was sure she had not failed. All through the years she had been teaching and training Helen to stand on her own feet. She believed that even without her help she would now be able to stand alone and carry on her great work in the world.

When the break came Helen felt numb with grief. To lose her greatest friend who for nearly fifty years had been eyes and ears to her, was a tremendous test of faith and courage. Was her faith in God strong enough to carry her through?

She decided on a plan of action. "We'll go to England again," she said to Polly Thompson who was still her staunch companion. "Then we'll go on to Scotland and see your brother. The manse is like a second home to me." She loved the friendly family feel of the Scottish manse in Bothwell where Polly's brother was minister. The family had given her such a welcome when she had stayed there with Anne on their holiday four years ago. The children were her friends and had learned the hand alphabet so that they could talk to her about all their doings. It would be good to go back there again.

So they set off, in November 1936, on their first voyage without Anne. As they walked the deck, Polly talked into Helen's hand of the sights and sounds on board.

"There's a flash of wings all round us," she said. "The birds are everywhere, but best of all I think are the tiny white sea-swallows, circling about the ship. What brave little things they are! Just think of those tiny defenceless creatures flying thousands of miles over the ocean, beyond any chance of rescue."

Helen Keller turned her sightless gaze towards the spot where she knew the birds were flying, and the sun shone warm and reassuring on her up-turned face. Somehow the thought of those tiny sea-birds flying out fearlessly into the unknown brought her new courage. It revived too her long-ing to travel, to see still more of the world, to carry to fresh places the torch of hope for the blind.

She began for the first time to keep a journal. Each day she jotted down the interesting things she had "seen" through Polly's observant eyes, and descriptions of people and events during their stay first in England and then in Scotland. How good it was to be welcomed again into the warm family circle at Bothwell! The whole family made her feel that she belonged, and that was the greatest comfort to her in her loneliness without Anne.

During her stay at the manse she went with her Scottish friends to visit the place where one of her heroes, David Livingstone, was born. It was wonderful to be allowed to touch his possessions which are still preserved there—the spinning-jenny at which he had worked; the sextant which had guided him through the jungle; the instruments with which he had saved so many lives. She felt with her fingers the plaster-cast of the shoulder bone which the lion crushed, and the worn Bible which he clasped as he died. Then Polly spelled into her hand these words which he had uttered: "I shall attach no value to anything I possess, except in relation to the Kingdom of Christ."

Standing there among the things that Livingstone had once possessed, she drew strength from the thought of his courage in giving all he had for Christ's sake. She resolved to go on bravely with the work God had given her to do.

★   ★   ★

That winter in Scotland gave Helen many new experiences to describe in the journal she had just begun to keep. To be taken down a coal-mine, for instance, was something very new to her. But the real red-letter day was the one just after Christmas when the entry in her journal began: "Today my head is buzzing with a letter that seems the call of destiny."

The letter contained a thrilling invitation—for her and Polly Thompson to go to Japan! They were asked to go there as guests of the Japanese Government to start a campaign for the blind— so far had Helen Keller's fame spread.

"Isn't it a wonderful opportunity!" she exclaimed. She explained to the equally excited family at the manse that the letter was from her Japanese friend, Mr. Iwahashi, a blind teacher whom she had met in New York two years before; he had begged her then to go out to Japan to start work for the blind but at that time Anne was too ill to be left so Helen had had to refuse. Now the invitation had come again and she was free to go.

She had always longed to meet the people of Japan—ever since as a girl of thirteen she had visited the World's Fair at Chicago and felt under her fingers the beauty of the Japanese bronzes exhibited there. Now she would be going not just to visit a country new to her but, as her Japanese friend had said, to open doors and let in the light for those "shut in a great darkness". As she thought of all she had heard and read of human need in the Far East where blindness is so terribly prevalent, she felt a tremendous longing to help. If only she could do something to stir the people of Japan to care for their own blind and deaf sufferers, how worth while this new adventure would be!

★   ★   ★

Three months later they were on their way, outward bound.

As their ship, the *Asama-Maru*, sailed out of San Francisco harbour through the Golden Gate, Helen remembered the first time she had sailed across this magnificent bay, in 1915. The romantic stories she had heard then of the ships that came from the Orient laden with jade and ivory, myrrh and frankincense, fascinated her. She had made up her mind that one day she would sail through the Golden Gate on her way to the Far East. The odd thing was that unknown to her Polly had had just the same idea—and now here they both were, setting sail for Japan!

"Another blue smile of a day in the blue Pacific," Helen wrote in her journal on 5 April, some days out at sea. Their cabin was like a garden of flowers, and throughout the voyage they were treated as Very Important People.

But the voyage was not all roses and blue skies. Helen had to work terribly hard, preparing at least a dozen speeches which the Japanese Government had asked her to make. Day after day she worked in her cabin from five in the morning till ten at night, until her head ached and her fingers were nearly numb with the effort of pounding out sheaves of notes on the typewriter. First thing in the morning when the sailors were swabbing the decks, she would walk up and down with Polly rehearsing the speeches she was going to make.

After all the hard work and preparation the tour was a tremendous success. Everywhere she went, blind and deaf Helen Keller was given a great welcome, for her message of hope for the blind and deaf was blazing a new trail in Japan. People flocked to see and hear her; they marvelled at the way in which she had conquered her own darkness and so was able to tell the people of Japan how to help the blind and deaf in their country.

★   ★   ★

That was the first of Helen Keller's tours round the world, campaigning for the blind. From that time she became a great traveller. In the ten years after the war she and Polly went on long trips to Australia, South America, Africa and Asia to plead the cause of those who lived in the dark.

As she travelled in all five continents, Helen realized how greatly the world had changed since the war. She felt a deep sympathy for the awakening peoples of the world, for their longing for freedom and independence. Her mind was always reaching out to try to understand other people's point of view, whether it was Jew or Arab, European, African or Asian. That was one of the most surprising things about her: the older she grew the more adventurous her mind became.

Her eager mind went on exploring because she had such an adventurous faith. "The Bible is the only book that reaches up to the times in which we live," she said. And she laughingly said that she had read her braille Bible so much that whole pages of dots had been worn off!

How she needed that faith and the courage it gave her in the days ahead! On one of her long trips abroad in 1946 the shattering news of a great disaster reached her by cable: "Arcan Ridge burned to the ground." Her lovely home in Connecticut, which she and Polly Thompson had built up together and where all her treasured books and papers were stored, had vanished overnight. All her possessions had gone, including her braille library and all her papers. Worst of all, the book which she was writing about her beloved teacher had gone up in flames. Into that nearly finished book she had poured her devotion and pride in the one who had taught her most. Now it was completely destroyed.

Still Helen Keller refused to be daunted. People trusted her, God trusted her, to go on with her work. She could not fail Him or her blind friends. In a matter of months she was starting on the book again to tell the world the story of her teacher who had made her own work possible.

A lovely thing happened when Arcan Ridge was rebuilt after the fire, for Helen Keller's friends in many parts of the world rallied round to help make it beautiful again. Many gifts for furnishing it came from her friends in Japan—inlaid tables and handsome chests, lamps and trays and carved ivory figures, and the Emperor of Japan sent her a personal present inlaid with gold and silver.

But the gift which appealed to her most of all was a Japanese stone lantern, nine feet high.

"We'll stand it in the garden and put a lamp inside it which we'll always keep alight," said Helen Keller.

It was so like her to be lighting lamps by which people could find their way in the dark. Polly Thompson said to a friend: "I think that that lighted lamp in the garden is a wonderful picture of the unquenchable spirit of Helen Keller!"

She was right. That unquenchable spirit is an inspiration to us all. For by the grace of God Helen Keller has triumphed over some of the greatest human handicaps. She has learned to conquer the darkness of the blind and deaf, not only for herself but for other sufferers throughout the world. And that is the kind of light that can never be put out.